LOVING GOD

WITH ALL MY
SOUL

To find yourself get lost in God.

Julie Ackerman Link

With All My Soul

© 2005 Julie Ackerman Link

Discovery House Publishers is affiliated with RBC Ministries,
Grand Rapids, Michigan 49501.

Requests for permission to quote from this book should be directed to:
Permissions Department, Discovery House Publishers, P.O. Box 3566,
Grand Rapids, MI 49501.

Also available in the Loving God Series:
  The Art of Loving God
  Loving God with All My Heart
For more information visit Discovery House Publishers on the Web:
http://www.dhp.org/

Cover Photo: Getty Images

Printed in the United States of America

05 06 07 08 09 10 11 12 / JRC / 10 9 8 7 6 5 4 3 2 1

Introduction

Throughout biblical history the crossing of the Jordan River represented an act of faith, a spiritual turning point, a new beginning with God. For me, crossing the Jordan required no faith. I was riding a bus, so I didn't even have to get my feet wet. It did, nevertheless, represent a turning point. As our bus climbed the barren hillside on the eastern side of the Sea of Galilee, our guide, Tony, pointed out military bunkers and explained why the land was so desolate. We were entering the infamous Golan Heights, the territory reclaimed by the Israelis in 1967, and the ground was still littered with landmines.

From a lookout point atop the mountain ridge, we gazed down on the farmland along the eastern shore of the Sea of Galilee. Before Israel gained control of the Golan, farmers working at the foot of the mountain had to use armored tractors to protect themselves from mortar shells fired from above.

Tony's comments about the present-day Jewish struggle sounded oddly biblical, and I felt as if I had just been walloped by a Bible released from a time warp. For the first time I thought of Scripture as being contemporary rather than just historical. God's work in the world did not end when He finished writing His best-selling book. He is still working, still writing people's life stories. But instead of recording them on leather scrolls, He's writing them on hearts and minds as He reclaims our souls, one at a time, and restores them for His glory.

During that first trip to Israel I realized that I was not just visiting a place where sacred things happened; I was visiting the people God put in that place to witness those things. Just as many features of the landscape have remained the same for centuries, so have the people. Their looks, their way of thinking, and their passions are much like the people of Jesus' day. Interacting with them gave me a new way of thinking about what it means to be a Christian. As such, I too am a citizen of a special kingdom—a spiritual kingdom. And I should be as passionate about that kingdom as the Israelis are about the nation of Israel.

As we bounced along in the bus one day, Tony gave us a brief history of the Jews and then asked this question: "What does it mean to be God's chosen people?"

From somewhere in the archives of my memory came an answer, which I blurted without bothering to think. "It means that all the nations of the world will be blessed through you," I said.

Immediately I wished I had kept my mouth shut because I didn't want Tony to think I was implying that the

Jews were to blame for the fact that not everyone in the world is blessed.

But Tony liked my answer. "That's exactly right," he said.

The answer was right because it came straight from Scripture, not from me:

> The Lord said to Abram, "Leave your country, your people and your father's household and go to the land I will show you. I will make you into a great nation and I will bless you; I will make your name great, and you will be a blessing. I will bless those who bless you, and whoever curses you I will curse; and all people on earth will be blessed through you." —Genesis 12:1–3

The last phrase indicates that all peoples of the earth will receive God's ultimate blessing—salvation—through Israel's Messiah, a descendant of Abraham. But it's also saying that people of faith, people who believe God, are God's ambassadors of blessing to others. We are to be living, breathing examples of our loving, compassionate God. Living in the righteousness of Christ, and in the power of the Holy Spirit, we are to be just, fair, good, honest, truthful, pure, and, above all, loving.

This Scripture, called the Abrahamic Covenant, is often used to focus on the blessings believers can expect to receive. But the Bible doesn't indicate that God's people are to become professional consumers of His goodness, or giant reservoirs to preserve it. The great crescendo of the passage is not what we're going to get; it's what we have to give. Believers today—just like believers living in the days of Abraham, Isaac, and Moses—are called to be God's channel of blessing to the world.

Channels only blessed Master,

But with all your wondrous power

Flowing through us, You can use us,

Every day and every hour.

MARY E. MAXWELL

WHEN THE BRIDE-TO-BE asked me to be in her wedding, I was caught off guard because I didn't know her very well. Assuming that she was going to ask me to function in some minor capacity, I managed to say, "Oh, that would be nice."

But then she said, "I'd like you to be a bridesmaid."

I tried to hide my surprise but must have been unsuccessful because she offered an explanation—one that was even more surprising than the invitation: "I'm asking people who will look good in the wedding pictures," she said.

I was too stunned by her response to consider it a compliment. Besides, I was already calculating the price I was going to have to pay for this unsolicited "honor." I tried to think of a polite way to decline, but I had not yet learned that skill, so I bought the dress, the shoes, the hair ornament, and I allowed myself to be used as a decoration in her wedding.

Being a bridesmaid was not new to me. In fact, I was beginning to wonder if the phrase "Always a bridesmaid, never a bride" was a prophecy concerning my future. Being close to the altar doesn't count in marriage. In all my experiences as a bridesmaid (twelve), the groom never decided at the last minute to leave with the woman in pastel instead of the one wearing white.

Despite my reluctant participation, the wedding worked for my good. As it turned out, I walked down the aisle with my future husband. Although the experience cost me more than I could afford, it got me two things money cannot buy: a godly husband and a good illustration.

Each of us has a past that is a scrapbook of things we

have and have not been chosen for, and recalling them will likely bring back the same emotions we felt at the time. Maybe you are like me and still can feel the humiliation of standing alone between two teams, the last person to be chosen for a game of softball. When it came to sports, I was always chosen last because my legs are too short for anything that requires speed, and I'm too much of a coward for anything that involves balls flying through the air. Other stories of rejection are more painful to talk about.

Too often we allow situations like these to determine our value. But assessments made by others on the basis of how well we meet their needs are faulty; they have nothing to do with our true worth or our real identity. But they seem right and real, so we believe them, not realizing that they are lies that keep us from hearing the voice of God.

- Fashion voices tell me that I'm a random arrangement of bones (that I must keep strong) and flesh (that I must keep sleek and solid), held together by skin (that I must keep smooth and supple) so that I will be a suitable hanger for the clothes they tell me I should wear.

- Government voices tell me that I'm a member of the important middle class (needed to fund projects and programs that keep privileged people in power).

- Advertising voices tell me that I'm a consumer who urgently needs everything I don't yet have.

- Wall Street voices tell me that I'm an investor whose task is to turn a little bit of cash into a lot of profit so that I can enjoy a few pleasures and not become a burden to society before I die.

- Technological voices tell me that it doesn't matter

who I am or where I'm going as long as I get there first and don't become obsolete on the way.

- Scientific voices tell me that I'm a fluke of nature whose task (ironically) is to improve the human species.

- Hollywood voices tell me that I'm playing a minor role in a plot so boring that everyone else's "reality" is more interesting than mine.

- Science and Hollywood join voices in an unlikely alliance, shouting these antiphonal reminders: Science shouts that I am here only because my species is the biggest bully, and Hollywood shouts back, saying that I will continue "being here" only if I am able to outwit my neighbors and become the last survivor.

If options like these are the only choices, we may as

well concede that evolutionists are right: human existence is just a contest in which the reward goes to the strongest and smartest, sometimes even the cruelest, but certainly not to the kindest or noblest. When life is reduced to competition, the best outcome we can hope for is to hold on for as long as possible and keep ourselves from being pulled apart in a tug-of-war between the competing interests of earth's greedy and power-hungry citizens.

Yet deep within us a voice whispers, telling us that our life is more than the accumulation of random opinions about our usefulness. But what is it?

What on Earth Am I Here For?

If sales are any indication of need, a lot of people are still trying to answer the question posed by the subtitle of Rick Warren's bestselling book *The Purpose-Driven Life: What on*

Earth Am I Here For? In the first year of publication, the book sold more than ten million copies, breaking the sales record for any book previously published. Although record-breaking sales are good news for the author and publisher, they raise a troubling question for the Christian community: Why are so many of us uncertain as to God's purpose for our lives?

The Bible declares that each of us is a unique individual designed by a loving and creative God, equipped with certain talents, fueled by particular passions, to fulfill a specific purpose, so why do Christians have such a hard time finding it?

Our job . . . is to teach our kids and grandkids to find their identity in themselves as God made them, rather than being swayed by brands and commercialized images—because in allowing themselves to be "branded," they . . . lose their true identity.

CHUCK COLSON

The generation that came of age in the seventies began tossing around the phrase "I need to find myself." Often it was used as a rationalization for behavior generally considered irresponsible. But somehow it seemed selfish to deny a person the opportunity to "find herself." In fact, it seemed as if the right to such a pursuit ought to be listed in the Declaration of Independence along with the right to life, liberty, and the pursuit of happiness, for how can one find happiness without first finding "self"?

Interestingly, the word *self* is closely related to the word *soul*. According to the *New International Encyclopedia of Bible Words*, "Soul is personal existence. It is the life or self of an individual."

Our souls contain the essence of our identity. One dictionary defines *soul* as "the immaterial essence, animating principle, or actuating cause of an individual life."

According to the Bible, the animating force within each human being is the breath of God. We are nothing but a clump of dust until God breathes His life into us. The breath of God in us is our soul, and it is our souls that make us distinct from one another and unique in creation.

> [H]uman beings are more than dust. In the creative act, God not only formed the human body but also "breathed into his [man's] nostrils the breath of life, and man became a living being" (Ge 2:7). Human beings are unique among living creatures, for the life that God created and with which he endowed them is a reflection of his own image and likeness

(Ge 1:26). The body may die, but our individual essence will never be dissolved.

—*New International Encyclopedia of Bible Words*

The word *soul* comes from the Hebrew word *nepes* and the Greek word *psuche*, which mean "breath." It is God's breath in us that defines our "self." Thus any attempt to know ourselves apart from God is doomed to failure.

But still we try. In fact, we try all sorts of things before turning to God—relationships, education, careers, possessions, stock portfolios, bank accounts, and sometimes even substances.

Early in life we define ourselves by relationships. As children, we are the offspring of our parents. Later we expand the definition of self to what we do. While we're in school we are students. Then we go on to become teachers, farmers, doctors, writers, artists, musicians, engineers, administrators, social workers, politicians, or a myriad of other occupations. Some of us become wives, and we change our names to identify ourselves with our husbands. Some of us also become mothers, and we become known as Mom. But even in the best of situations, these titles are temporary. All of them can be taken from us; none provides a permanent identity. And when we're stripped of titles and tasks, and sometimes even relationships, we're no longer sure who we are.

Whenever we go through a period of transition, it's common to experience a crisis of identity. After focusing on one task for a long time, we feel lost when it's finished. If we

> If I look to other relationships to define who I am, I can't become who God created me to be. My most important relationship must be the one between God and me.
>
> RIKA DIEPHOUSE

identify ourselves by what we do, the feeling of being unnecessary is tantamount to having no identity. This is especially true if what we do is connected to what we are called and who we are related to.

Being a mom, for example, carries with it both a name and a job description. So it's no wonder that someone who has been called "Mom" for years starts to question who she is when she no longer hears the urgent call of a toddler yelling "Mommy," or the demanding whine of a teenager pleading, "Mom!"

Due to a series of unrelated circumstances one year, I lost my place in my family, my business, and my church. During that time I had to answer some difficult questions: Which part of my identity transcends the titles I hold and the tasks I perform? Who am I when I'm separated from people I love, places that are familiar, and positions that give me meaning and significance?

Some of us keep our fragile selves propped up by avoiding situations where loss, failure, or rejection is likely. But in doing so we may miss God's plan for our lives. One of those places may be precisely where God wants to display His glory in us.

Consider Moses. After a failed attempt at delivering his fellow Jews from Egyptian slavery, Moses dashed off to the desert and hid for forty years. When God showed up and told Moses to go back and try again—this time in God's power and timing—Moses was less than enthusiastic. In an attempt to disqualify himself from the assignment, Moses raised the question of his identity.

Who Am I?

When God announced to Moses that he had been chosen to lead the people out of Egypt, Moses tried to argue his way out of it by saying, "Who am I to lead these people?"

His response was somewhat disingenuous in that forty years earlier Moses was already thinking of himself as Israel's deliverer (Exodus 2), but God graciously ignored that detail.

God could have given His frightened friend a pep talk about how well equipped he was for the task, but He didn't. He could have recited Moses' life story, reminding him of how he had been spared from death at infancy, reared in the king's palace, and prepared in the sheep fields of Midian to learn—by practicing on sheep—the difficult task of leading difficult people. But there was no "You can do it if you try" talk from God. God was more concerned about Moses knowing who God was than in bolstering Moses' self-confidence.

In a response much like those we hear from politicians determined to "stay on message," God chose not to answer the question Moses asked. Instead He told Moses what He wanted him to know: In essence He said, "Moses, you're asking the wrong question. Before you can find out who you are, you need to find out who I am."

Moses needed confidence in God, not in himself, and for that reason he needed *not* to be reminded of who he was but to find out who God was. And that is where all questions of identity begin.

Who Is God?

If you want to have a little bit of fun the next time you get into a theological discussion and someone asks, "Who is God?" say "I am."

Of course, you want to say this only if the other person

doesn't have a mouthful of hot coffee to spew all over you. When the person regains composure, you're likely to hear a somewhat sarcastic response, like, "And just how long have you known that you are God?"

That's your cue to say, "I didn't say, '*You are* God,' I said, 'I am.'"

If you're clever enough (I'm not), you could prolong the conversation (and the confusion) and perhaps become famous for creating a theological version of Abbot and Costello's classic comedy sketch about baseball: "Who's on First?"

Or you could quote Exodus 3 and explain that "I AM" is the name God gave Himself when Moses wanted to know what to call Him.

For a long time I wondered why God would call Himself by such a peculiar name, but I'm beginning to understand its significance. One of the first lessons of grammar is that a sentence needs only two things to be complete: a subject and a verb. So when God says His name is "I AM," He is saying that He is complete. He is matter, and He is motion. He is everything there is, which is everything we could possibly need.

God expanded on the meaning of His name throughout His encounters with humans. In fact, in a series of brief interactions with Moses, God led him through three stages of revelation. First, God said His name was "I AM." Then God added two words, saying, "I am the LORD." Finally, by adding two more words, God made one of the most stunning pronouncements of history. He said, "I am the LORD *your God*." The creator of the universe made Himself personal. He affirmed to Moses what He had told Abraham:

> "I will establish my covenant as an everlasting covenant between me and you and your descendants after you for the generations to come, to be your God and the God of your descendants after you." —Genesis 17:7

In addition to making Himself personal, God set Himself apart from all other gods by choosing to reveal Himself. Contrary to what we sometimes think, the Bible is not a "how-to" or "self-help" book; it's an autobiography. It is God telling His life story so that we can know Him, and in knowing Him know ourselves as He knows us. (See 1 Corinthians 13:12.) We are all characters in God's autobiography, and our lives are pages in the unfolding drama of redemption.

The Bible says that God created us in His image, so a flawed image of God will keep us from knowing ourselves.

This means, if we have created a mental image of God out of the dust of our own experiences, we have constructed a false God.

Experience alone leads to wrong conclusions about God. Bad experiences lead us to think that God is mean, uncaring, and impossible to please, or that we are simply unlovable. Good experiences lead to the false conclusion that God just wants us to be happy no matter what we do or how we live, or that we are just getting the good that we deserve. All such self-conceived ideas about God need to be tested by Scripture.

The prophet Isaiah painted one of the most simple yet beautiful word pictures of God found in the Bible: He who "measured the waters in the hollow of his hand" and "with the breadth of his hand marked off the heavens," "comes with power" yet "tends his flock like a shepherd"

(40:10–12). Isaiah depicted God as being both strong and gentle, both above us and with us.

But even creation with its vast oceans and majestic mountains, and all of Scripture with its histories, poems, and prophecies, could not adequately represent God. He had one final word to say about Himself, and that word is *Jesus*.

Who Is Jesus?

Jesus left the comfort and safety of heaven to put flesh on God's bare-boned answer to Moses' question "Who are you?" God said of Him: "This is my Son, whom I love; with him I am well pleased" (Matthew 3:17). Among the details that Jesus added to explain His Father's name, and to expand on what it means to bear the name "I AM," are these:

I am the Alpha and Omega, the First and the Last.

I am the way, the truth, and the life.

I am the bread of life.

I am the light of the world.

I am the good shepherd.

I am the resurrection and the life.

—From Revelation 22:13; John 14:6; 6:48; 8:12; 10:11;

11:25

God added to the testimony of His Son, revealing even more about His identity, in the writings of the apostles. To believers living in Colosse, Paul expanded on Christ's list of "I ams" with this amazing "He is" list:

He is the image of the invisible God, the firstborn over

all creation. (Colossians 1:15)

He is before all things, and in him all things hold

together. (1:17)

He is the head of the body, the church. (1:18)

He is the beginning and the firstborn from among the
dead, so that in everything he might have the
supremacy. (1:18)

Then, in a stunning statement that is nearly lost because
it is one of several in the passage, Paul writes:

God has chosen to make known among the
Gentiles the glorious riches of this mystery,
which is *Christ in you*, the hope of glory. (1:27,
italics added)

After hearing everything that Paul said about Christ,
the Colossian believers came to the surprising words
"Christ in you."

People living in that part of Asia believed in gods that
were impetuous and impersonal, who hovered above the
people, lived in man-made temples, and demanded gross

self-sacrifices from their followers. The notion of a God who would come down, make a personal sacrifice, and take up residence in His followers, well, no one had ever heard of such a thing.

Later in the letter, Paul adds another unheard of idea: "For *in Christ* all the fullness of the Deity lives in bodily form, and *you have been given fullness in Christ*, who is the head over every power and authority" (2:9–10, italics added). Not only was Christ in them; they also were *in Christ*.

One of the mistakes we make in trying to determine God's purpose for our lives is that we reduce it to decisions related to what we should *do*: where we should go to school, where we should live, whom we should marry, what career we should pursue, and what job we should take. Then we compound our faulty thinking by falsely assuming that right choices will lead to fairy-tale endings.

While "what to do" decisions are important, the Bible indicates that they are secondary. The first question each of us must ask about ourselves is "Am I in Christ?" If the answer is yes, the next question is "Who am I in Christ?" Regarding this, Jesus made two important statements: speaking of Himself, He said, "the Son can do nothing by himself; he can do only what he sees his Father doing, because whatever the Father does the Son also does" (John 5:19). And of His followers, He said, "apart from me you can do nothing" (John 15:5).

Before we can *do* anything, we must be *in* Christ.

In a Regent College chapel service, Professor Paul Stevens said, "God has called you, and God is calling you. . . . You and I are not left to invent the meaning of our lives. We are not left to figure out what we're on earth for. Or to find out who we are simply by introspection."

The apostles wrote about our calling with these words:

We are called *into* God's kingdom and glory
(1 Thessalonians 2:11–12) *by* His own glory and
goodness (2 Peter 1:3–4) *for* the praise of his
glory (Ephesians 1:12) *to* share in God's glory
(2 Thessalonians 2:13–14).

Stevens went on to say, "God has called you into relationship with Himself . . . before we are called to do something, we are called to some*One*. . . . We won't find out who we are without finding out Whose we are. Never forget Whose you are, because that is who you are."

What better news could there be than finding out that we are God's children?

How great is the love the Father has lavished on
us, that we should be called children of God!
And that is what we are! —1 John 3:1

I Am God's Child

When I answered the late-night phone call, I had no idea
what lay ahead. My father was in the emergency room after
falling at home and injuring his eye. The next morning I met
Mom and Dad at the eye surgeon's office.

When the doctor started to take the bandage off Dad's
eye, Mom said, "You probably don't want to look, Julie." I
agreed, and stood just outside the door, thinking I was a
safe distance.

It seemed, however, that everyone in the office
wanted to see what I did not want to look at. Some
crowded into the small examining room. Others stood
outside the door near me. Like I said, I thought I was
safe. But even though I could not see my dad's injured
eye, I could see the horror in the eyes of those who did.
One kind nurse—trying to comfort me I'm sure—put

her hand on my shoulder and said—over and over—"Poor Dad, poor Dad, *poor* Dad."

Sometimes too much kindness can make a person weak, and that's what happened to me. The more pity I received, the weaker I became. The weakness hit my stomach first, and I felt powerless to hold down all the coffee I'd been drinking. But just in time the feeling of "losing it" moved to my head and then to my eyes. When the lights started going dim I quickly found a chair and sat down. At once a comforting blanket of darkness covered me, and I felt relieved to no longer see or feel anything.

But then one of the nurses broke my shell of protection. "Are you okay?" she asked. "Can I get you something?"

"Cold water might help," I said.

She brought me a cup of ice water, and by the time the

doctor had once again covered Dad's eye, I was feeling well enough to listen to the bad news.

Somehow in the fall Dad had not only ripped off the cornea transplant he'd received several years earlier, he'd also managed to mangle the retina. The doctor offered little hope that he'd be able to see with that eye again, but said he couldn't be certain until after surgery.

Outside the room, my mom got a little teary-eyed. "I just want things to be the way they were yesterday," she said.

"I know, Mom," I said. "But nothing's going to be the same for a few weeks."

She cheered up a little at the idea that this was only a temporary setback, and then we wheeled Dad over to the surgical wing of the medical center where we waited some more.

Later I was able to think about the many emotions that had overloaded my circuits that day. I thought about all of those strangers looking inside my father's head, and I realized, metaphorically, that I knew very little about what went on in there. I thought about how little time I had spent getting to know my dad, and I wondered if I was afraid to find out about him for fear that I would learn more about myself than I wanted to know. Then I considered my reluctance to get to know God, and I realized that it too has to do with wanting to avoid the truth about myself.

As I thought about the fall that had left Dad sightless in one eye, I thought about The Fall (capital "F") that has left all of us spiritually sightless. And then I thought about a heavenly Father who wants nothing more than to have His children look into His eyes and see who He is so that we can stop hiding who we are.

Get Lost in God and Find Yourself

Only when we lose ourselves in Christ can we begin finding our true identity. Jesus said, "[W]hoever wants to save his life will lose it, but whoever loses his life for me will find it" (Matthew 16:25). The Greek word translated "life" in this verse is *psuche*, the same word that is translated "soul" in the great commandment (Mark 12:30), and which also means "self." In other words, when we lose our "selves" for Christ and His good news, we find out who we are meant to be.

What, then, does it mean to lose our "selves"?

"You are such a loser!" These words are meant to hurt, and they do. The old "sticks and stones" response is little comfort. It fails to acknowledge that not all injuries are physical. Some of the most serious hurts are those that damage our *psyches*, or souls, and name-calling is an assault on a person's soul. God designed us to be truthful, so our "default setting" is to believe what we hear, and when we hear ourselves being called a disparaging name, we tend to believe it.

It hurts to be called a loser because it says that we are worthless. But it's a lie. Now that I am older and wiser, I have a ready answer. The next time someone calls me a loser, I'm going to say, "Thank you so much for the compliment. That's the best thing you could say about me. Jesus said I couldn't find my life without losing it, so I am losing myself to find Jesus. I am losing my anger, bitterness, and hatred, and I'm finding God's mercy, forgiveness, and love."

That, I believe, is what it means to lose my "self."

When people say, "I need to find myself," I think if they really search and find themselves, they may be quite disappointed. It's in finding God that we know ourselves.

PHIL KEAGGY

But as we find out more about who God is, we make a troubling discovery about ourselves: We find out the truth that we've been trying to avoid since infancy. We learn that we are *not* God, that the world does *not* revolve around us, and that we must relinquish the right to rule because we are filled with all kinds of nasty thoughts and desires that are not at all godlike.

In fact, the first identity crisis each of us faces is finding out that we are *not* the center of the universe. This is a hard truth to accept after the blissful days of early childhood when everyone around us behaved as if we *were* the most important creature on the face of the earth. The transition is long and difficult, and there are many setbacks. Once we are removed from center stage, we have many choices to make, and the truth is, we make many bad choices. These send us scurrying back to the center where we try again and again to take up residence and to reorder the world to revolve around us. All the while we pretend that we aren't really there and claim that it's not where we want to be because we know it's not where we belong. Yet we still think, subconsciously at least, that it's the only safe place to be.

Being bumped off center stage is traumatic, but it's only the beginning. Finding out who and what we're *not* clears the stage for us to see who we really are. The early scenes are reason for despair, and many stomp out in anger. But those who

Humility is facing the truth. It is useful to remind myself that the word itself comes from humus, earth, and in the end simply means that I allow myself to be earthed in the truth that lets God be God, and myself his creature. If I hold on to this it helps prevent me from putting myself at the center, and instead allows me to put God and other people at the center.

ESTHER DE WAAL

pay attention to what the Playwright is saying, and who
persevere to the end, are compensated beyond measure.

ACT ONE: I Am a Wretch

Some people don't like singing the hymn "Amazing Grace"
because they don't like referring to themselves as a wretch,
as in the phrase, "that saved a wretch like me." Frankly, I
don't see the big deal. God even referred to Jacob, whom
He loved, as a worm (Isaiah 41:14). The good news of the
gospel is that even wretches and worms can be loved by
God and redeemed for a noble purpose. (See Romans 5:8.)

With God, being honest about who we are leads to a
relationship, not rejection. Jesus proved this in His
encounter with a woman of not-so-noble character. Tired
from a long journey, Jesus sat down beside a well in a town
that most self-respecting Jews would go the extra mile to

avoid. Then He started a conversation with a woman no self-respecting Jew would speak to.

When Jesus asked the woman for a drink, she expressed surprise that He would speak to her (John 4:7–9). Jesus indicated that He wasn't who she thought He was, and she expressed interest in knowing who He was (vv. 10–12). Instead of identifying Himself, however, Jesus told her what He had to offer: water that would satisfy her thirst (vv. 13–14).

In a surprising reversal, the woman then asked Jesus for a drink (v. 15). When Jesus asked her to go get her husband, she explained that she didn't have one.

Instead of attacking her for what He knew was an evasive answer, Jesus commended her for telling the truth. Then He told her something about herself that she wasn't eager to have known: that she'd had five husbands and was living with a man she wasn't married to (v. 18).

The woman then recognized that Jesus was a prophet (interestingly, not because of what He said about Himself but because of what He knew about her, v. 19) and steered the uncomfortable discussion away from herself by bringing up the impersonal subject of where to worship (v. 20).

Jesus changed the subject back to something personal—from "where" to worship to "who" to worship (vv. 21–24). The woman, trying again to make it impersonal, expressed faith that the Messiah would one day explain everything (v. 25).

Seizing the opportunity the woman opened up by mentioning the Messiah, Jesus told her who He was with a simple "I am" statement: "I am he," He said (v. 26).

Note how Jesus kept the conversation going. He didn't tell her how bad she was. He just kept increasing her thirst (like salt) for more knowledge about Himself. He turned a

daily chore into a spiritual lesson. He didn't condemn her
for who she was or what she was doing; He gently led her to
discover who He was and what He could do for her.

When the disciples rejoined Jesus, the woman returned
to the village. Later in the passage we learn that many in the
town believed in Jesus because of the woman's testimony
(v. 39). However, it wasn't what Jesus said about Himself
that convinced them; it was the truth He spoke about the
woman. She returned to her neighbors urging them,
"Come, see a man who told me everything I ever did,"
(v. 29). After meeting Jesus, she was no longer ashamed of
who she was. She had met someone who knew her
intimately but had no desire to condemn her.

Seeing ourselves as we are is the first step toward
becoming all that God designed us to be.

One reason I believe the Bible is true is that it doesn't

whitewash the leading characters. Even the best of them are revealed to have flaws. Unlike humans, God does not cover up the faults of His favorite people. It is quite foolish, then, for me to think that He will help me hide mine. I shouldn't be surprised. After all, Moses warned the Israelites that their sin would surely find them out (Numbers 32:23). This passage is often used as a scare tactic to keep people from sinning, and maybe it has some effect. But still we sin, so perhaps it should also be used to encourage confession. After all, being the first to admit our own sin is better for our souls than waiting to be accused of it by someone else. The New Testament gives further support to this idea: "Therefore confess your sins to each other and pray for each other so that you may be healed" (James 5:16).

Scripture is more than a little discomforting on this subject because it says that we should reveal what we want to conceal (our sin) and conceal what we want to reveal (our good deeds). In His most famous sermon Jesus said, "Be careful not to do your 'acts of righteousness' before men, to be seen by them. If you do, you will have no reward from your Father in heaven" (Matthew 6:1).

Honest confession about who we are keeps the cause of Christ moving forward. Denial, cover-up, and secrecy sap the energy of Christian communities and keep people focused on the past.

With God, confession is the first step to a relationship, not to rejection. Imagine if it were the same with us. Imagine if we learned to interact with sinners the way Jesus did. He had a way of making people understand that His concern was not to call attention to their sin to condemn them for living badly, but to redeem them for a better way of life.

ACT TWO: I Am a Witness

Identity theft is on the rise, say those who claim to know. But how can identity be stolen? I realize that my social security number, my credit card numbers, and my bank account numbers can be taken and used fraudulently. But these numbers do not add up to my identity. I am more than a collection of numbers connecting me to my earthly "riches," and anyone who implies otherwise is committing another kind of identity theft by reducing me to the sum of my bank balance.

Another form of identity theft is even more insidious because we perpetrate it against ourselves. It's a form of spiritual suicide that we commit when we try to be someone other than who we are. To become like someone else who is already beautiful or popular or talented or intelligent seems easier than discovering our own gifts and abilities, passions and desires, and finding a place to use them.

As a writer, I struggle with this. Whenever I sit down in front of my computer, I try to make my words sound like Henri Nouwen or Anne Lamott or Philip Yancey. They don't. If anything, my words sound more like those of an impatient preacher. I want to be soothing, not scathing; amusing, not accusing; inspiring, not indicting. I wonder if the prophet Jeremiah wanted to write like David, the singer and songwriter, or like Moses, the historian. Or was he content to speak in the style and for the purpose that God assigned him even though his message was unpopular?

We cannot be an effective witness for God if we insist on using someone else's voice or talent or experience.

Contrary to what I believed for many years, being a witness does not mean memorizing the plan of salvation so I can explain it to strangers; it means telling others the truth about myself and my personal encounter with God. It means being able to say "I was," but now "I am." In the words of the hymn writer, "I once *was lost,* but now *am found, was blind,* but now I see."

One summer I worked at a Christian camp, and one of our "duties" was to go to a nearby resort town and do street evangelism. Well, drop me off in a resort town and I knew how to shop, but expect me to stop strangers and "witness" to them about God? I don't think so. To be a witness a person has to have seen or experienced something. The Bible is clear about that. One of the Ten Commandments is "do not bear false witness." Standing on those lakeside streets I felt like a false witness, but not because I wasn't a Christian; I was. I believed God. I trusted Christ. I did not deny my sinfulness and was grateful to accept forgiveness. But I did not have the kind of dramatic conversion experience that I thought was needed to make a convincing case for God.

I trusted Christ at age eight, so sin hadn't yet had a chance to reach the fullness of its ugly potential; the "was but am" aspect of my testimony wasn't very compelling.

Since then I have learned that my testimony doesn't have to be dramatic. My witness is the simple story of my life. It's my first-hand account of how God is taking the "me" that He created and is gently and lovingly transforming and restoring it to its full potential for His glory. Slowly but surely He is turning me from a clump of clay to a work of art.

The Greek word translated *workmanship* in Ephesians 2:10 is *poiema*, from which we get the English word *poem*. In other words, *we are* God's poem, His artistic expression. *We are* God's good work!

I still feel the residual guilt of those early failed witnessing attempts. But I am somewhat consoled when I remember that

Moses didn't start his public ministry until he was eighty years old, and even Jesus didn't start until He was thirty. Looking back, I believe that I was being required to do something I was not equipped to do. I was being sent to "go, tell" before doing the prerequisite "come, follow." I had not yet seen what God had done, was doing, and could do in my life. I didn't realize that I had not simply been saved *from* the consequences of sin but also saved *for* the cause of righteousness.

On my computer screen next to this document is an e-mail I just received requesting that I write a two-to-three-sentence description of myself for a Web site. How timely that I am given the opportunity to answer a form of the question "Who am I?" when that's the subject I'm trying to write about. The request includes these guidelines: "Leave out the marital status/family stuff and the academic degrees. Keep it light and fun."

Since Jesus described Himself metaphorically, I've tried doing the same, and this is what I've come up with:

> I am a magnet for factual debris. Like Pigpen in the *Peanuts* comic strip, who lives under a cloud of dust, I live under a cloud of disconnected fragments of stories, observations, experiences, and information. My role in the universe, like a crime scene investigator, is to figure out how these seemingly unrelated fragments fit together to reveal truth; then I form them into a shape that will help me (and hopefully others) see that truth more clearly.

The way I am made in the image of God is that I take dust (in my case words and information) and mold it into something useful (i.e., knowledge and wisdom). I don't need a big budget, a big staff, or a big audience to accomplish this. I only need eyes that can see God, ears that can hear Him, and a heart that is willing to look for God in every experience and to reveal God in every encounter. (Oh, and I also need the patience to let God decide if, when, how, and where to use my service.)

Poet T. S. Eliot wrote:

Where is the Life we have lost in living?

Where is the wisdom we have lost in knowledge?

Where is the knowledge we have lost in information?

The cycles of Heaven in twenty centuries

Bring us farther from God and nearer to the Dust.

—From "The Rock"

My assignment from God is to reverse the process Eliot wrote about. I am to arrange the particles of dust that come to me in a way that points people to God. But that is all I can do. The rest is up to God. My life motto, based on 1 Thessalonians 1:5, is: *I can put words on a page, but only God can breathe life into them.* Unless God breathes life into "the work of my hands," which I pray that He will do, everything I write will be a worthless idol.

Jesus, fill now with your Spirit
Hearts that full surrender know
That the streams of living water:
From our inner selves may flow!

MARY E. MAXWELL

ACT THREE: I Am a Worshiper

One week before Jesus was crucified, a woman named Mary poured a whole bottle of expensive perfume on His head and feet. Then she did something even more remarkable: She wiped His feet with her hair.

Not only did Mary sacrifice what may have been her life's savings in this extravagant act of worship, she also sacrificed her reputation. Respectable women in that culture never even let down their hair in public, much less do anything as audacious as Mary did. To worship Jesus, Mary was willing to be considered immodest, perhaps even immoral. She knew that true worship was letting down her hair and making herself vulnerable. In churches today, many of us think of worship as putting our hair up and making ourselves unapproachable.

Some people attend big churches because they can hide. They feel safe when they remain unknown. But this contradicts the purpose of being part of a church. A church is only a church when it's a safe place to be known—a place where we can reveal our weaknesses and find strength, not where we have to conceal our faults to appear strong.

Worship is the one task for which we all are chosen. Life on earth is our great rehearsal, and Jesus is our great worship leader. In the prelude to the greatest worship service the world has yet experienced, Jesus ate the Passover meal with His friends. Writing about that evening, the apostle John said, "Having loved his own who were in the world, he now showed them the full extent of his love" (John 13:1). This is John's account of that evening:

> When [Jesus] had finished washing their feet, he put on his clothes and returned to his place. "Do you understand what I have done for you?" he asked them. "You call me 'Teacher' and 'Lord,' and rightly so, for that is what I am. Now that I, your Lord and Teacher, have washed your feet, you also should wash one another's feet. I have set you an example that you should do as I have done for you. I tell you the truth, no servant is greater than his master, nor is a messenger

greater than the one who sent him. Now that you know these things, you will be blessed if you do them. —John 13:12–17

The disciples still did not know how radically different their lives were going to be before the night ended, but this was certainly an indication that the world they lived in was being overturned, in much the same way that Jesus, earlier that week, had overturned the tables of those who were corrupting worship in the Temple. Jesus was redeeming worship, and He was about to do it by making Himself the sacrifice. Like witnessing, worship has to be personal, and it has to be done willingly. True worship is an act of love. It's giving up our "selves" in service for others.

> The greatest, most beautiful expression of our creativity is to find a way to give ourselves.
>
> MICHAEL CARD

GRAND FINALE: **I Am a Bride**

As the sun set behind us, a line of weary hikers, including myself, moved slowly up a rocky Turkish hillside toward the ruins of a church built to honor the martyred apostle Philip. Upon reaching the site, we gathered inside the octagonal structure to take Communion—to remember the death of Jesus in the place where one of His first followers had been savagely executed.

Our teacher, Ray VanderLaan, spoke of the new covenant Jesus announced to His disciples the night before He died. Linking the customs of the Passover cup and the Jewish marriage cup, he explained that Jesus, in saying to His disciples "This cup is a new covenant in my blood," as He offered them the cup of salvation, was, in essence, telling the disciples that He wanted them to be His bride. In taking the cup, the disciples accepted His proposal.

While meditating on the amazing concept of the church being the bride of Christ, I recalled another Turkish location, Antioch, where followers of Jesus were first called Christians, or "Christ ones." Like a bride, Christ's followers were called by His name.

As I took the cup, I had a hard time swallowing the juice. I thought of the places I had been—the other worship settings I had seen. Those who worshiped pagan gods came to their ceremonies dressed in white but went away covered in bloody stains from their own self-mutilating sacrifices. In contrast, my God used His own blood to wash away my stains and present me pure and spotless, like a bride dressed in white, adorned for her husband. I was overwhelmed with gratitude that Jesus wanted me as His bride and would take the risk of letting me be called by His name.

I think about how careful I am about how my own name is used. I think about the projects I choose to work on—and the ones I don't because I would be embarrassed to have my name attached to them. I think about the people I associate with; I choose them because I am not ashamed to be seen with them and not afraid of what they will say about me.

Then I think about all the unlikely people God has chosen to be called by His name. Suddenly the distinction between humans and God is unmistakable. Like grooms choosing brides, and brides choosing bridesmaids, and captains choosing players, we humans choose people who make us look good. But God chooses people He can make good.

God chooses those judged "losers" by the world's standards and makes them the beneficiaries of His riches. He chooses the lost and leads them home. He chooses those who are unclean and unkempt and does such a thorough clean-up that they become a bride adorned for His Son:

> Christ loved the church and gave himself up for her to make her holy, cleansing her by the washing with water through the word, and to present her to himself as a radiant church, without stain or wrinkle or any other blemish, but holy and blameless. —Ephesians 5:25–27

In his vision on the island of Patmos, the apostle John saw four living creatures seated around God's throne who kept repeating the same few words. "Day and night they never stop saying: 'Holy, holy, holy is the Lord God Almighty, who was, and is, and is to come'" (Revelation 4:8).

To be honest, I used to think, *What a boring existence!* But I don't think that anymore. Instead I think about what it's like spending time with someone I love, or doing something I love to do. I don't want to leave; I don't want to stop. I want time to stand still.

That must be what it's like for the special creatures in John's Revelation. I try to imagine the scenes they have witnessed from their position around God's throne. I consider how amazed they must be at God's wise and loving involvement with wayward earthlings. And then I think, *What other response could there be? What else is there to say but "Holy, holy, holy"?*

Is it boring to say the same words over and over? Not when I'm in the presence of the One I love. Not when I'm doing exactly what I was designed to do.

Like all creation, each of us is designed to glorify God. So life will be an amazing adventure if we remain in Christ and live and love in the power of His Spirit for the glory of the Father. For God created us, knows us, loves us, and has a special purpose for us.

Loving God with all my soul means rejoicing in every breath I take, because the air that gives pleasure to my lungs and life to my whole body reminds me that every moment is a gift from a living and loving God who created me in His likeness, who called me to bless the world on His behalf, and who allows me to bear the name of His perfect Son.

Praise to the Lord!
O let all that is in me adore him!
All that hath life and breath,
come now with praises before him!
Let the amen sound from his people again;
gladly forever adore him.

JOACHIM NEANDER